I0435922

"The whole place could go up in smoke in ten minutes. That's the charm of Los Angeles"
-William Burroughs

"You can check out, but you can never leave"
-Eagles, "HOTEL CALIFORNIA"

AN EARLY SOUTHERN CALIFORNIA morning in July and I pull into the familiar beach parking lot that I used to spend my everydays at 5 years ago, living in my van. My old unofficial spot near the Mexican Fan Palm tree was vacant. But there was no Suzanne and 5 cats in big pickup truck with wood cabin on back. Nor was Carol present in her camper van (I would learn 2 weeks later that Carol had died last month). Earl from Oregon and his big RV were gone too. Other once familiar rigs were nowhere to be seen either. There were a few fresh faces, but the absence of the regular crew made it feel strange and lonely.

I thought about how everyone had moved on from "The Lot", and yet here I was, returning to it…

Nevertheless, there was a familiarity which felt OK. The mighty Pacific was only a few hundred yards away, and I looked forward to what would turn out to be a daily baptismal ritual of body surfing, underwater immersion, and bitterness bleaching of the mind = a much needed cleansing from the previous three and a half months of mental misery living under a bridge in Northern California…

Even though the lot was depleted of the once regular vehicular vagabond comrades, there were still many friends here, and this was reason enough for returning to Angel City.

NIGHT TIME BACK IN THE DAY WE WOULD GO FROM "THE LOT" TO THE VENICE STREETS
WHERE WE WOULD POST UP FOR THE NIGHT. SUZANNE LIKED PARKING IN FRONT OF ME
AND CAROL WOULD PARK BEHIND ME. THEY SAID THEY FELT SAFE WITH ME IN THE
MIDDLE. WHEN I LEFT TO GO LIVE IN NORTHERN CALIFORNIA, I REMEMBER FEELING
MASSIVE GUILT FOR BREAKING UP THE SAFETY NET THEY HAD COUNTED ON…

I HAD CHECKED OUT OF LOS ANGELES 5 years ago as it was
clear in my mind that this place was going to collapse,
and collapse quick. Going North, somewhere smaller and
more sustainable was clearly the way to go as this place
was headed towards complete and catastrophic
destruction. But now, upon returning, L.A. Is more active
and vibrant than ever. More energy and chaotically
controlled activity permeated throughout. As I looked
around, I had to embarrassingly admit that over the last
5 years, it turned out that the only thing that had ended
up really collapsing was the relationship with the
woman I had been living with up North; the chaos and
confusion of an over congested city of 10 million people,
is no match for the conflict and clashing of 2
individual ego's....

HANDS TO HEAD, FEELING DEFEATED BEING BACK IN L.A.

THE NEW HOSTILITY OF LOS ANGELES

With more people, comes more chaos. As L.A. Now seemed more crowded than ever, there was added agitation in the air. Returning to the city, I witnessed a ramped up hostility all around, and oftentimes I found myself caught in the middle of it.

HOSTILE GROUNDS #1

The large two floor Santa Monica public library consists
of 1/3rd "regular" patronage, 1/3rd homeless shelter, and
1/3rd county jail general population. You have a mix of
houseless individuals, many trying to get some daytime
shut eye, then you have actual library patrons doing the
library thing, and then there are fresh out of county
thugs mad-doggin around, trying to stir shit up.

SITTING AT THE TABLE across from me is a young Latino
dude, minding his own biz, listening to music on his
headphones. A few hours go by and a young white dude
sits across from the Latino, at the same table. Looks
immediately get crossed, and "that thing" happens that
lights the initial spark, and words are exchanged.

From this point on, every 5 minutes the white dude would

start talking shit under his breath. "*FUCKIN FAGGOT...I'LL*

BEAT YOUR ASS FAGGOT." The Latino guy would talk back

some, shake his head some, and try to laugh it off some.

But the white dude wouldn't relent.

"C'MON, LET'S GO OUTSIDE RIGHT NOW FAGGOT!"

The air was thick with tension that just kept building.

After about 20 tense minutes of this intermittent back

and forth shit talk banter, the white dude gets up, steps

towards the seated Latino and starts kicking him. The

Latino gets up, pushes him away, then the full on fist

fight proceeds down the aisle, eventually making it's way

into the Art's and Literature section...

Meanwhile, I spring up, waiting for an opening where I can break the fight up. I hesitate jumping in right away because I secretly want the Latino kid to get in some decent shots, as he was more the victim of this whole mess.

But the white dude manages to get Latin's shirt up over his head while teeing off shots to his face. When it looked like Latin was about to go down, where the white guy would have pounced on top of him, I realized my opening was now. I jumped in, separated the two, declaring "FIGHTS OVER...ENOUGH!"

The white dude looked at Latin and said, "i beat your ass dude." He then quickly split, and then the bumbling security guards, who had been busy waking up homeless people, finally showed up.

The Latino kid sat back down, feeling somewhat defeated. He explained to me that his reluctance to fully engage in the fight was because he was on probation. I felt guilty upon hearing this, knowing I could have broken up the fight sooner, but I had let it go on hoping he would engage more.

Nevertheless he thanked me repeatedly for stepping in. I told him that he was smart and that he did good. This raised his spirits some.

BACK AT THE BEACH parking lot I got my suit on for my daily ocean immersion and proceeded across the lot to the sand. It was a windy day and a surfboard fell off a guys truck. A passerby on a bicycle tried to warn the guy

that the board was about to fall, but it was too late as

the board smacked the pavement. K L U N K !

The surfer got out of his truck and motioned to the

passerby on the bike to *"get over here motherfucker!"*

The dude on the bike looked confused. He paused, but then

smartly kept on riding. The surfer turned to me and

asked, "did that asshole just knock my board over, or was

it the wind?" I told the guy, "I think it was the wind."

The guy responded, "You know, it doesn't even matter bro,

any reason to pound someone..."

"L.A. MAN... THIS TOWN......
I BE TRIPPIN' OFF THESE PEOPLE!
THEY GOT A LOT
OF ISSUES...
A LOT OF ISSUES
NOW I REMEMBER
WHY I LEFT
HERE..."
-Regular
Library
Patron, also
recently
returned to
L.A.

HIPSTER HOSTILITY

My old stomping grounds of Venice became hard to hang in. Two of the main streets were now hardly recognizable; littered with ridiculous useless hipster high priced "t-shirt shops" and expensive, trendy looking eateries with names like "FLAKE" and "FEED".

Around the corner from a street which is heavily populated with houseless people living in tents on the sidewalks is a cafe called "CAFE GRATITUDE".

g r a t . i . tude -"readiness to show appreciation for and to return kindness."

Maybe the gentrifiers "mean good"; more likely they don't know any better and perhaps don't realize the people living on the streets and in their vehicles have been here for many years before they landed here, and will be here for years after they leave. From the hipster demeanor they seem caught up in their own artificial scene, uninterested in the history and true character of the turf they are temporarily calling home.

CAFE GRATITUDE

STORIES BEING EXCHANGED ABOUT WORKING IN HOLLYWOOD

VENICE STREETS

STORIES BEING EXCHANGE ABOUT OLD VENICE

STRUCTURAL HOSTILITY

The hostility of the structural scene may be the worse form of over aggressive behavior yet. The one story homes I remember were now demolished and rebuilt into architectural visually nauseating 2 or 3 story "domains" which now go for over a million dollars.

Meanwhile more and more parking signs have sprung up saying, "NO VEHICLES OVER 7 FEET"..."NO PARKING BETWEEN 2-4 A.M." All an obvious attempt to create a parking loophole violation in order to kick out the houseless RV and vandwellers who have been living here for years. The irony is that they are now allowing enormous 50 foot tall sunset blocking eyesore structures to be erected, while disallowing vehicles over 7 feet to be parked.

I thought about making fliers and starting a mock campaign to change the name of Venice to "VENICEAN HEIGHTS", as everything was getting taller and flakier, while the history, flavor and feel of Old Venice was near dead.

ATTN: PETITION REQUEST / SIGN BELOW

WELCOME TO VENICEAN HEIGHTS!

LET'S CHANGE OUR NAME TO REFLECT THE NEW LUXURY LANDSCAPE WE ARE ERECTING

AND THE TREND SETTING SILICON BEACH VIBE WE ARE CREATING!

VENICEAN HEIGHTS RERESENTS THE CHANGE THAT "VENICE" DESERVES! IT'LL STILL BE

"FUNKY", BUT CLEAN, TRENDY AND FRIENDLY FUNKY!

PLEAESE SIGN HERE TO LIE 'VENICE' TO REST AND BRING V-HEIGHTS TO LIFE!

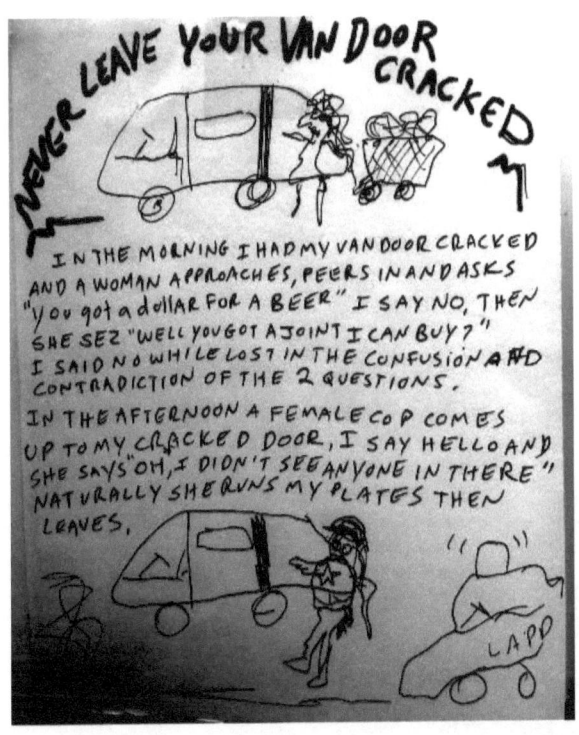

IN THE MORNING I HAD MY VAN DOOR CRACKED AND A WOMAN APPROACHES PEERS IN AND

ASKS, "YOU GOT A DOLLAR FOR A BEER?" I SAY NO, THEN SHE SEZ, "WELL, YOU GOT A

JOINT I CAN BUY?" I SAID NO WHILE LOST IN THE CONFUSION AND CONTRADICTION OF

THE ? QUESTIONS. IN THE AFTERNOON A FEMALE COP COMES UP TO MY CRACKED DOOR.

I SAY HELLO AND SHE SAYS "OH, I DIDN'T SEE ANYONE IN THERE." NATURALLY SHE

RUNS MY PLATES AND THEN LEAVES.

IN THE PUBLIC LIBRARY MENS BATHROOM I WAS SEATED DOING MY BIZ. THE GUY IN THE STALL NEXT TO ME WAS VIOLENTLY PUKING. ANOTHER GUY WAS LOOKING IN THE MIRROR RECITING LOUD RELIGOUS BABBLE WHILE TURNING THE AIR DRYER ON REPEATEDLY. I THOUGHT ABOUT HOW THESE MUST BE THE WORST CONDITIONS TO HAVE TO LISTEN TO WHILE PAINSTAKINGLY PUKING YOUR GUTS OUT.

HOSTILE GROUNDS #2

As I was leaving the public library for the day, a guy came up to the second level and asked the desk if they would call security, as two guys were pushing him around downstairs in the courtyard. For some reason he then proceeded back to the stairs, to descend down back to the courtyard. I suppose he thought security would meet him there by the time he got down and would then diffuse the situation allowing him to make it past the thugs without harm.

Meanwhile, I was right behind him, descending down the same stairs. I saw the 2 thugs in the courtyard, waiting for the guy to return. One of them looks up and says,

"LOOK, HE'S COMING BACK DOWN...*AND HE'S BRINGING HIS PARTNER WITH HIM!*"

I quickly realized I was being perceived as "the partner". So now it would be an even 2 on 2 fight. Time stopped for a moment in my head as I thought to self "really? Now how in the FUCK is this happening???"

"HE WENT AND HE GOT HIS PARTNER...HERE THEY COME!"

Down below was a short 5'5 Latino bulldog lookin thug and his buddy was a black guy with a nasty fucked up looking eye. They were both fresh out of County Jail most likely, having that pent up energy most caged animals get when locked up for a stretch.

The guy in front of me reached the courtyard, naturally no security in sight, and immediately gets confronted by the bulldog who proceeds to shove him around, egging him into engaging in a fist fight. After some quick turns and swift steps the guy eventually was able to push past him and then dart by the black guy with the nasty fucked up eye. Having missed his opportunity to throw down, the bulldog then directs his attention to me, "the partner".

As he begins mad-doggin me, hopping around ready to throw, he also maintains a certain distance which tells me there's a 10% doubt in him that maybe I'm not "the partner".

I grit my teeth, roll eyes inside head while tellin myself "don't tangle and get yourself kicked out of this place because of this dumbfuck pug and this dumbass chance encounter." I knew I could increase the doubt in him if I just kept walking and avoided direct eye contact. Though at same time I readied myself in case the little dog decided to go for the bone regardless.

Meanwhile I see the 2 bumbling security guards racing up the stairs, oblivious to the reality that all this shit was going down right here...

As I walk pass the still unsure hopping around bulldog, I feel so goddamn pissed and frustrated, and at this point I almost hope the pug lurches towards me. I t,think back to what the surfer in the parking lot said the other day, "any reason to pound someone", and now was surprised to be feeling the exact same way...

THUGS FRESH OUT
OF COUNTY
MAD DOGGIN AT
THE PUBLIC LIBRARY

BACK AT THE LOT the whole wrongly being mad-dogged thing kept bugging the shit out of me. I laid down in my van and decided to crash it off.

After a few minutes I was awoken by some sort of commotion at the other end of the lot. It was a crazy black woman yelling shit. Her rants seemed to be directed towards the Latino's.

Every Friday afternoon, a large group of Latino's come down to The Lot with their classic low rider cars. They park them all next to one another and then sit on the bike path ledge and hang out watching the people walk, ride and skate on by.

Things hit the breaking point when the black woman

shouted out the three words in which there would be no turning back from:

"FUCK ALL MEXICANS"

With this much show of force, the Latino's could not let a statement like that go unanswered, crazy schizo lady or not.

Several immediately got up off the ledge and headed towards her while verbally firing back. Then a few nearby black guys decided to chime in and stand up for the black lady.

It now looked as if BLACK VS BROWN was officially ON.

"Jesus Krist". I shook my head and lay back down as it seemed there would be a few moments of verbal sparring before anything physical would happen. After a minute or so I glance back up to see if the showdown had progressed any further. The absurdist turn it took made me fully get up and out of my van to see how in the hell this one was going to unfold.

What I immediately noticed was one of the black guys standing on top of a moving SUV truck driven by one of the Latino guys. The truck began speeding through The Lot, swerving back and forth as it tried to shake the guy off the top. But the black guy was able to maintain his balance, still standing on the SUV roof. So the driver decided to employ another tactic.

He sped up even more, but this time he suddenly slammed on his brakes. This sent the rooftop surfer flying off the SUV,. He soared several feet in the air before landing on the hard concrete ground.

Huge gasps of horror were heard by the now many onlookers. It was as if we had just seen someone be potentially delivered to their deathbed.

Yet somehow, amazingly, the black dude emerged from the hard pavement fall, seemingly unscathed.

This seemed to only fuel the fire on both ends. The Latino, while able to shake him off the hood, didn't end up inflicting any damage from the speed up and stop tactic. The black guy on the other hand, emerged

heroically, now bragging how he had somehow survived
the hard landing.

"HAH-I'M AIGHT-DIDN'T DO SHIT TO ME-CAN'T EVEN TAKE ME OUT

WITH YOUR GODDAMN SUV BITCH!"

As I watched cell phone calls being made by each group,
speed dialing in re-enforcements, a few cops showed up on
the scene and did the same. Their re-enforcements arrived
first as within minutes helicopters were hovering
overhead and a flurry of new parole cars were racing
towards The Lot. All of which ended up preventing the
potential race war from occurring, which was all the
result of three words shouted by a schizophrenic crazy
lady…

<u>OCEAN HOSTILITY</u>

Even the ocean had it's bouts of Hostile. The tide was coming in much further than I'd ever seen, and the waves had become intense at times.

It was a Saturday afternoon and a German Vegetarian beer fest (only in Santa Monica) had overtaken The Lot. It was frustrating being in the same lot, yet denied entry to the tented off area a dozen feet in front of me, where 45 dollar tickets were being charged for freshly tapped brew and fake sausage made with tofu.

As the festivities ended at 6pm, I suspected many of the drunk patrons would make their way down to the beach and likely some into the ocean.

I was already fully emerged in big Pacific when a cute
gal fresh from the German fest had opted for a dip and
happened to be wading my way.

"What are you...like a swimmer?"

"I'm a body surfer."

"Oh, can you show me your technique?"

She came closer, real cute chick, and even though
submerged in salt water, the German beer permeated
heavy. I noticed she didn't have a swimsuit on, as she had
gone right in wearing her summer dress. As we got into it,
and I began "showing her my technique", naturally a
heavy and hard set came rolling in-one after the other-
major crashing down hard and high waves, forcing us to
dive under, one after another, after another, after
another.

It became pretty intense and eventually panic kicked in on her end as her dress began to seriously weigh her down while the waves continued to come in stronger.

"Can you help me make it to shore???"

I grabbed her hand and swam her in, but I think we were caught in a rip current that kept pulling us back. We had to pause our pursuit to shore and dive under the continually strong oncoming waves. It was a bizarre and unrelenting set, with a rip current thrown in for good measure.

Finally I got her in. She appeared lost and we roamed the shore for her friends. Eventually a tattooed guy with a

Black Flag T-shirt waved her down, and I waved her off,

half wanting to ask Black Flag where his inked up ass

was when his girlfriend was near drowning...

PASSING BY

Living in a van you are forced to interact, observe, and inevitably get caught up in the lives of others, passing by.

Throughout the day there will be a number of men who pass by my van, seemingly beaten down, lost, looking tired, unsure, dazed, confused, bedraggled, gone; sometimes semi-hopeful but be-speckled by some checkered past or maybe just a no-nothing past of missed opportunity, a left when should've turned right, or submerged in self doubts which plagued any potential progress forward. Sometimes they are in pairs, one lost soul having just met another walking along the same patch, exchanging much needed human commnunicato between one another.

Weaving reasons, excuses, resources, tall tales, hopes; fortunes to be had and hardships to forget. A verbal release that is often just as good or better than a smoke/sniff/inject or drink, which many will turn to anyway before the day is out.

PASSING THRU

There's also a good number of passing through travelers. From a busload of hippy gals, to that one kind of character that only America can produce..

TOMMY had a long suburban type SUV with bedding in back and 3 pitbull mixed pups roaming about. He was coming from Florida with his two kids to drop them off at his ex-wife's for a few weeks in Northern California. The ex-wife had drove down to meet him in L.A. and then take the kids to Disneyland for the day with her new boyfriend. Tommy declined the invitation to go along to Disney for the day, and instead opted to hang out here in The Lot and pound away cans of Coors Lite till nightfall.

The next day Tommy would follow his ex-wife up to the Bay area, where the kids would hang out with Mom, and Tommy would hit San Fran where he said he was going to meet up with a buddy and do some cocaine. They would white nostril tromp around the city for a few days and probably try to hook up with some women. Tommy was looking forward to doing some cocaine, but not so much the women part.

"We always seem to end up with these real troubled women who all have major, major issues..."

Tommy pointed out several items he was wearing: an ACE bandage around his knee, a large necklace with a pendant of some sort, a few rings, and a new tank top.

"ALL FREE! We hit the Walmarts, Targets, and all other big box stores that we pass through while traveling. Freeing the china babies I call it!"

Tommy went on to explain how he goes into the big box stores with his 8 year old daughter, who will bring along a bag, and together they ransack the place, putting whatever they want into the bag, and then leaving, sometimes smiling at the security guard as they exit.

"In and out in 90 seconds. I explain to my daughter how these places all exploit their workers, mostly children who make all their profits. So we're taking away from their profit margin! We're freeing the China babies!"

Tommy was a trip.

"TOMMY"

Los Angeles is a mix of routine and randomness. You can
have a solid routine down, yet randomness will always
enter and interfere with your situation, for better or
worse.

Interrupting my daily workout routine was a man around
my age, all fucked up - face a mess and bandaged, while
his arm was in a sling. He said it was a skateboarding
accident and he just got out of the hospital. He was lost,
trying to get to the pier, but had walked the wrong
direction. He waited patiently for me to finish a set of
lunges, then asked for a ride to the pier. He said he'd
pay me 5 bucks. He was thin and said he was suffering
from 2 forms of cancer, both he was informed were too
late to do anything about. Nevertheless he was going to
start chemo next week for the slim chance it would work

in this late stage. He seemed genuine and I wondered if the skateboarding accident was a case of recklessness; risk taking knowing he was going to exit soon anyway. Living out last minute thrills.

I told him I was sorry for his condition.

"It's alright...I've had a good life."

He was extremely thankful for the ride when we reached the pier and he exited my van. He never gave me the five and I didn't ask for it.

DRIVING A DYING MAN

AROUND MIDNITE A QUARRELING
COUPLE SLEEPING ACROSS FROM ME
IN THEIR SUV. THINGS GET HEATED,
BUT AT TIMES COMICAL AS I HEAR THE
GUY SAY "WELL i HAVE HOPES AND DREAMS TOO,"
THINGS THEN SETTLE FOR A STRETCH,
BUT THEN PICK UP AGAIN, AS THE GUY
FINALLY REALIZES WHAT THE PROBLEM
IS WITH HIS GIRLFRIEND. HE LET'S OUT
A FEROCIOUS ROAR AND WITH THE UTMOST
SERIOUSNESS, HE PROCLAIMS:

YOU ARE THE DEVIL... WITH HORNS!

HOSTILE GROUNDS #3

Back at the public library I sat across from an old man at a table. Me and the old guy were the only ones at the table, while several other tables surrounded us with various library patrons seated.

The old man had an old laptop computer and a number of large books on ancient Egypt were stacked near the laptop. At some point, I began hearing "sounds" emanating from his computer. A lot of "ooohs" and "ahhhs" delivered by a female sounding voice. I quickly discerned that hardcore porno sounds were coming out of his computer. I whispered gently to the old man, "Hey, I think your audio is on." He fired right back at me: "NO IT'S NOT!"

Nevertheless he investigated further, picking up his laptop and holding it to his ear. He then barked at his laptop, saying to it: "Why you dirty sumumabitch!"

The dirty old man then proceeded to push buttons trying to find the volume control. But as he fumbled around, the porno sounds only intensified. Now all the other tables surrounding us could hear the building female orgasm.

I had to close my own laptop so people wouldn't think the sounds were coming from me. Meanwhile it was interesting to watch the reactions from others. Almost all the women who were seated at nearby tables got up and left the area, seemingly embarrassed and annoyed. Some of the men covered their faces, holding in their laughter. Other men attempted to ignore it, but that became near impossible after a while.

The dirty old man was now turning his laptop upside down and all around, trying to find a mute button. He tried turning his computer off, but he had hit so many buttons by this point that his machine had frozen up and would not turn off.

Finally the man just held his laptop in his arms, completely defeated, while the sounds of a woman having sex carried on, now louder than ever...

I DECIDED TO CHIME IN, again, as I had an idea. "Why don't you try taking out the battery?" Rather than bark back at me like before, he replied, "well, that's a good idea."

He turned the machine over, fidgeted with the battery lock switch for a moment, and then successfully removed the laptop battery. The orgasm stopped.

He was relieved, as were the patrons surrounding us. Only one woman returned to our section.

The dirty old man closed his computer, picked up one of the ancient Egypt books, flipped through it for 10 minutes, then got up and left.

I pondered about the hostile nature created by female sexual sounds permeating throughout what was supposed to normally be a quiet and calm public space.

BACK AT THE BEACH PARKING LOT I was getting ready to take on the ocean when I noticed a regular car dweller whip into the lot. He had a small black station wagon with the front hood completely missing. Smoke from the center of the engine would shoot out every time he gunned it hard. He seemed to enjoy gunning it hard and having the black smoke shoot out of his hoodless wagon. He appeared more than a bit schizo as well.

On this occasion he was in prime form. He whipped into the lot and gunned it hard, black smoke shooting straight up and out. He then started yelling out the window to a pair of guys walking by.

"GET THE FUCK OUT OF MY WAY ASSHOLES!"

He then swerved in their direction for a quick second, pretending he would run them down. When he got to the other end of the lot, the section where I park, he stopped his wagon and settled into a space. He left it running though, occasionally giving it gas so a shot of black smoke would shoot out.

Meanwhile, the two guys at the other end of the lot saw that he was parked, and decided to make their way over to the hoodless wagon. Uh-oh.

When they got there, hoodless was still in the drivers seat, apparently unaware of his approaching visitors. The two guys rushed the car and began yelling at him, then pulled him out of the car and started beating him.

Hoodless went down and I raced over there fearing the guy could get stomped on hard. When I got there, hoodless was talking smack from the ground, denying he did anything wrong while throwing "jesus" in here and there. One of the guys lifted him up by his hair and you could feel the temptation to heavily smack the schizo around some more as there just seemed no way to bring the guy out his delusional denial and admit he was a total asshole.

After much back and forth bickering and continued denial from hoodless, the two guys I think realized that they were dealing with a madman and no further beat down would change his warped reality. They left the guy on the ground, told him to go fuck himself, and walked off...

HOSTILE GROUNDS #4

Down at The Lot, around 7 am, there was an odd young couple bickering at one another near the restrooms. She was a large heavy set white girl with a massive black eye. He was a short and thin black guy.

"IT'S ALWAYS ABOUT YOU!" the big white girl shouted.

The black guy replied, "OH, OKAY, SO I GUESS I'LL JUST GO KILL MYSELF SINCE YOU DON'T LOVE ME ANYMORE!"

Big white proceeds to lock herself in one of the bathroom stalls out of frustration. From inside she ferociously bangs on the bathroom door while yelling "UGGHHHH AHHHH FUCKKKK.. I'M SO SICK OF YOUR SHIIIIIT!"

She then suddenly emerges from the bathroom and full on charges towards her boyfriend. The guy swings, clocking her a few times on her already black-eyed face.

I've been watching the whole show while approaching the scene and at this point I verbally intervene, "CUT THAT SHIT OUT - ENOUGH!"

He stops and they face each other. I would've intervened further had it not been such an absurd sight. This large white gal, who now had her huge fists clenched at her sides, threatening her little black boyfriend how she'll kick his ass all the way to Tibet if he swings at her again. It was hard to tell who needed protecting here.

The bickering continues. He again says he's going to go off and kill himself since she doesn't love him anymore. She goes from bitching to balling to eventually begging. She absurdly drops to the ground, gets on her knees, and begins bowing down to him, while repeating: "YOU ARE GOD. I AM NOT WORTHY."

Someone had already hit the emergency 911 call button, and I notice the cops entering The Lot. Things seemed to have now calmed down some, so I turned and walked off. As I looked back, just a second before the cop car pulled up to the couple, Big White suddenly sprang up from her begging position and jumped on Little Blacks back. Maybe Little B had taken some judo in the past, because somehow he was able to curl his own body forward and toss her mammoth body over his shoulder. THUMP. She landed hard

on the pavement as the police got out of their car and
approached.

What a goddamn life I thought.

FOR MONTHS AN SUV WOULD PARK in the morning hours at The Lot. A white couple would sit inside, the guy at the wheel and the gal in the passenger seat. I would walk by them on my way to the restroom to take my early morning piss.

One morning I hear some commotion as I'm heading toward the latrine. Things are thrown out of the SUV. The girl gets out and begins circling the truck with a skateboard held high above her head. She then takes the board and WHACKS the side of the truck. The man yells and the gal again holds the skateboard high as a weapon toward the potential retaliation from the guy.

But the guy fires up the SUV and revs up the engine. He yells out a future threat: "YOU BETTER WATCH YOUR ASS BITCH!" He then peels out of The Lot.

The woman gathers up her belongings, clothes, bags, and a purse, then sets the skateboard down on the ground, and skates off on the bike path heading South. I watched her roll off until her image disappeared. I imagined how she was skating away, into a brand new life. A new chapter perhaps.

The next morning I see the same SUV enter The Lot. The same guy is in the drivers seat. The woman from yesterday, who had skated off into the sunset, is seated in the passenger seat...

THREE MONTHS HAD PASSED since I first rolled back to "The Lot", swearing to self I wouldn't be here longer than 3 weeks. But for some reason it took me 3 weeks to realize…uhhh…I don't exactly have anywhere to return to.

I suppose I could live out my days in this chaotic cesspool surrounded by the beauty, both natural and unnatural. Surrounded by the ugly, both manufactured and bred. The ocean as my savior. The characters as my study. The madness as my inevitable downfall.
You can check out but you can never leave.

THIS place is like a steoreotypical blond - pretty on the outside, yet shallow and empty on the inside....

YOU CAN CHECK OUT was written and drawn by ELI ELLIOTT

THANKS TO STEVE X, DAVE B, ALEXIS Z, MIKE G, 212 PIER, AND THE

PACIFIC OCEAN.

WEB LINKS TO CHECK OUT:

www.Elienation.com

www.Elienation.ORG

www.AbsurdistVideoArt.com

www.ColdFusionNow.org

If you would like to contribute towards self publishing costs

for more physical copies to be released of this book, and the

several future books on the burner, my paypal is

EliDork@yahoo.com

Thanks for reading.